DREAM DIGGING GUIDE 2

DREAM DIGGING GUIDE 2

Discover
THE HIDDEN BELIEFS
IN YOUR
Dreams

Janet S. Wahl

MindBalance LLC

Published by MindBalance LLC
Albuquerque, NM 87120
www.dreamdigging.net

Printed in the United States of America

19 18 17 15 16   1 2 3 4 5

ISBN: 978-0-9963346-3-1 (ebk)
ISBN: 978-0-9963346-2-4 (pbk)

Human Brain Waves Diagram/Chart/Illustration by Legger (49733789) and *Sleep Graph* by Artellia (43331606) used with permission from Dreamstime.com. Photos: OpenClipArt.org, Pixabay.com

The ThetaHealing* technique is a registered trademark of Vianna Stibal, ThetaHealing Institute of Knowledge.

All comments in the dream group are from actual people. Names have been changed to protect the privacy and safety of the dreamer. Any resemblance to actual persons, living or dead, is entirely coincidental.

The information in this book is intended for educational purposes only. No content in this book is to serve as medical or psychological advice. It is not therapy. Please contact a medical professional immediately for any condition that requires a diagnosis or medical or psychological attention. The author disclaims any liability arising directly or indirectly from all of the practices in this book. In the event you use any of the information in this book for yourself or others, which is your constitutional right, the author and publisher assume no responsibility for your actions.

Library of Congress Control Number: 2016917322

Cover design: The Scarlett Rugers Design Agency, http://www.scarlettrugers.com/
Editorial and page design: Holly Monteith Inc., http://www.holly-editorial.com/

For
Dreamers and ThetaHealers
who continue to evolve through belief work

Contents

Introduction

Fertilizing carpets.
Meat rotting in my handbag.
Sirens blaring all night.
Running and hiding: I murdered someone!
Phantasmagoric light!

Infected with fear, anger, confusion, or horror, or sometimes blessed with absolute joy, sounds and images materialize in our dreams. Fragments without plot, shape-shifters crossing time and space, characters growing young, all vaporize into thin air as we try to capture them with words. Where are they conceived? Why do they appear in dreams?

Originating in our subconscious minds and unedited by our waking consciousness, dream images speak truths that our waking minds spin and revise to serve our public façades. Dreams are a rich resource for healing. They are unique to each dreamer. Hence, dream dictionaries, although entertaining, may be inaccurate and misleading. What is meaningful for one dreamer may well be meaningless for another.

Montague (Monte) Ullman, MD (1916–2008), created the Experiential Dream Group (1999) to help dreamers explore the meanings of images and stories in dreams. His unique method allows the dreamer rather than an outside authority to be in control of the exploration. No group member may press interpretations, advice, or judgments on the person sharing a dream. The imaginative associations of the group are offered to the dreamer as projections to enrich the broad spectrum of possible meanings, something the individual dreamer can do only on a limited basis. However, not everyone has access to an Ullman dream group in close proximity to where she lives.

This book guides an individual dreamer, who may not have the benefit of a dream group, to explore the meaning of a multi-layered dream and unearth some underlying unknown beliefs. Once identified, the ThetaHealing® technique (Stibal 2015), a form of hypnosis, provides a method to change limiting beliefs, which is the topic of *Dream Digging Guide 3*. These processes enable a dreamer to resolve some of the conundrums and quandaries of life.

Enjoy my Weird of the World stories that led me to dream work and the ThetaHealing technique. Learn how to discover the messages and beliefs that lurk beneath the images in your dreams through a systematic approach based on the complete Ullman process for dream work described in *Dream Digging Guide 1*. The charts and examples may help you process your own dreams for greater understanding.

Join an online dream group, listed in the "Online Resources" section, that uses the Ullman method.

An Important Message for Readers

The information in this book is intended for educational purposes only. No content in this book is intended to serve as medical or psychological advice. It is not therapy. Please contact a medical professional immediately for any condition that requires a diagnosis or medical or psychological attention. The author disclaims any liability arising directly or indirectly from all of the practices in this book.

Most of the dreams included in this work are my own. The names of people in the dreams, if they are real in waking life, have been changed. The names of the participants in the dream groups have also been changed to protect privacy. Privacy is an absolute requirement to ensure trust and safety in dream work.

However, Monte Ullman and Claire Limmer are real people, who deserve attribution for their work.

one

The Weird of the World and Beyond

Behind all seen things lies something vaster;
everything is but a path,
a portal or a window
opening on something other than itself.

—Antoine de Saint-Exupéry, *Wind, Sand and Stars*

Noises and Visions

"What is that noise, Daddy?"

My small body waited at the fence row where my father was chopping alfalfa to make silage for the cows. The tractor pulled the huge chopper, both engines roaring. Of course, I could hear the chopper and the tractor, but there was another similar noise, nearly as loud.

"It's the chopper," he replied.

"No, the other noise."

"It's the tractor," he said. I guessed he couldn't hear that other noise. I had heard it so many times, sometimes at night, sometimes during the day. I don't remember how old I was when I first heard it. Often it was in my dreams, a big scary noise next to a big black hole. I waited fifty years to learn what it was.

Grandpa

I grew up on a Midwestern farm in the 1940s and 1950s with five brothers and sisters. As the oldest, I helped take care of the younger ones. I often wished I lived in town so I could walk to school instead of taking the bus. In high school, our social structure consisted of two groups: town kids were suave; country kids were smart. As soon as I got my driver's license, I organized and drove my siblings to their activities so I could attend more and more of my own events, many with the town kids. If I fulfilled the taxi runs, my folks more readily allowed me to use the car—enlightened self-interest, perhaps.

Grandpa and Grandma, who spoiled us, lived two and a half miles up the gravel road. We loved to go visit because Grandma always had freshly made cookies and candy. Early one morning, my brother, age three or four, in his kiddie car, and I, about five or six, on my tricycle, pedaled up the gravel road to Grandma's house. We had gone halfway when our great uncle enticed us with a swing ride at the country school. On our way again, he ratted us out to our folks, so they picked us up in the car before we completed our journey. Au contraire to the adults, we did not consider our journey as "running away from home." My dad picked us up, and after our second attempt, the subsequent punishment prevented us from doing it again.

On our birthdays, Grandpa gave us a big bag of groceries filled with our favorite foods not yet labeled as "junk." Grandma baked a birthday cake studded with M&M candies and put it on a crystal pedestal cake plate—until my brother and I broke it playing a forbidden game of basketball in the house.

During the next decade, Grandpa had heart trouble, but he refused to go to the doctor even as he grew weaker and more confused. Evidently the oxygen was no longer getting to his brain. One Sunday afternoon, sitting in his recliner, he said, "Time to put the horses in the barn." He had not had horses for dozens of years. That October, he was gone.

On the morning of his funeral, the minister directed the family into a pew in the front of the church. Speaking with us privately, he droned, "You remember what a wonderful man he was and how much he did for you."

"What does he know about Grandpa? That guy doesn't have a clue. He doesn't know about the birthday bags. Why doesn't he just shut up? He makes me feel worse!" I gazed at the wristwatch Grandpa had given me for confirmation a few years earlier, and my dam of tears broke.

After the service, I had the responsibility of driving my brothers and sisters to the cemetery. Tears blurred my vision. "It's so unfair that my parents get to ride in the big black car following the hearse while I have to drive. After all, I'm younger than they are." My lungs convulsed.

"Why can't we ride, too? There is plenty of room," I asked my dad when he poked his head in the window to see if I was okay. Only sixteen, I had just obtained my driver's license.

"Someone has to drive our car. We can't just leave it here at the church," my dad replied. I had to assume the care of my siblings. My parents could no longer afford my childhood.

On a cloudless day two weeks later, my best friend, Barb, and I were walking along the main street in our small town during the school lunch hour. It was the thing to do: bolt down the edible parts of hot lunch and then hike downtown. If we had money, we bought potato chips for a dime or a candy bar for a nickel.

It was ten minutes to one; we had to scurry back to beat the tardy bell. As we raced along, we passed my grandfather, wearing his blue-and-white-striped denim overalls, approaching us on my left next to the parking meters. I sucked in my breath and kept on walking. He passed us looking at the sidewalk. Terrified yet curious, I turned to catch another glimpse but only saw the parking meters. Seeking verification, I spluttered, "Barb, did you see that man we just passed?"

"What man?" she replied.

"Ohhhhhhh, I'm not mentioning this!" putting the incident out of my mind. Forty years passed before I knew why I had seen him on the street that day.

In Company of the Weird of the World

I was in my forties and teaching in Westchester County, north of New York City, when Pat and Dave invited my husband and me to dinner with colleagues. We had been friends for ages. Pat had invited a few more friends, one of whom was George. As we were enjoying the delicious food and entertaining stories, the conversation turned to the supernatural. George recounted his past-life regression.

"So who did you go to, George?" I asked.

"Tracy. She's a great psychic who does past-life regressions."

Fueled by a few glasses of wine, mild competitiveness ensued. Pat related that her grandmother had died a few months earlier. She had lived with Pat's mother and dad, up on the third floor of their home. Pat, who had been devoted to her grandmother, climbed up to her grandmother's room two weeks after her death. Grandmother was sitting in her chair smiling. "Hmmm," I thought, "so I'm not the only one," and reported meeting my dead grandfather on the street. By the end of the night, I had contact information for Tracy, the psychic and hypnotist whom George had seen.

Past-Life Regression

"Should I call Tracy? Is it true that people have past lives? Can I trust George's judgment? What am I doing?" buzzed my thoughts as I called Tracy for an appointment. She gave me a date, a time, and her address on Third Avenue in New York City. She took only cash—two hundred dollars.

I was nervous the day I drove the thirty miles from home into the city. The crime rate was high in the 1980s; people were regularly mugged. Unwanted window washers intimidated drivers stopped for a red light. Unsavory characters walked the streets, particularly on the far West Side. Even though I was going to the East Side, I had no idea if the neighborhood was safe. Carrying cash wasn't such a good idea, so I wore my electric blue Amelia Earhart jumpsuit with a multitude of pockets so I could dispense with the handbag. No one would notice a walking neon bag!

I rang the buzzer to a walk-up; the door opened into a dark stairway. "Come on up," Tracy called.

At least I have the right place, and she expects me. Is this a hoax? Am I walking into a robbery? Still apprehensive, I trudged up the stairs.

When I saw Tracy, her long hair and smile, it was clear I had nothing to fear. The two hundred dollars went from my pocket to her hand, and she invited me to sit in her comfortable recliner. "What question or issue do you want answered today?" she asked. As my marriage was beginning to fray, I asked her why I was having such difficulty. Tracy told me we would go to the past life that was influencing this one, and she would guide me into deep relaxation. "Imagine you are going down a set of stairs. I am going to count from ten down to one, and when I get to one, you will be in the life that is most influencing this life.

"Ten . . . nine . . . eight . . . you are getting closer and closer to the life influencing your present life. Seven . . . six . . . going down, down, further down . . . closer and closer . . . five . . . four . . . down, down closer to that life . . . three . . . two . . . one. You are there now. What do you see?"

I had trouble "seeing" anything. There was nothing there.

"Where are you?" Tracy asked. "Are you inside or outside?" I had no clue; it was black. Again, she counted me down the stairs. We must have repeated this at least four times.

At last I saw darkness filled with little lights. "What year is it?" Tracy asked. "Look at your feet. What type of shoes are you wearing?" I looked, but I had no shoes because I had no feet and no body. An empty sausage casing like jellylike tentacles was floating in the place of my body. I loved it; it felt so good—I wanted to stay in this place forever.

Tracy, somewhat frustrated, counted me down again, attempting to get me to another "real" lifetime. "Where are you? Is it day or night?" she asked.

"It's daytime. I'm in a ripened wheat field. It's all beige, no color anywhere. It's desolate. There's a small house in the middle of the field."

"Go into the house," Tracy said, relieved. I entered. It was a simple cottage with a bed, fireplace, and chair. "Are you alone or with someone?"

"I'm alone."

"What happens next?"

"I'm looking down from the ceiling."

"Go to the next major event. What happens?"

"There's a man. It's my grandfather in this life," I said. "I just stay on the ceiling. I don't want to come down."

"Go to the last day of your life. You see how you died. You'll be an observer, viewing it without feeling any pain or sorrow, and give me a report."

"I don't know. I guess I died in that house; maybe someone molested me. I stay on the ceiling."

"What was the most important lesson of that lifetime?" Tracy prodded.

"I don't know." My chest sank in failure and disappointment.

We went to a few more lives, one in Italy. I was married to my current husband. He carried a briefcase, wore a suit, and commuted to work. I waited for him in front of our brick fireplace. He was not the artist he is in this life. Apparently we had been together more than once.

In another life, I was a mother with two children. We floated in a boat fishing for dinner. The boat slipped under a rocky outcrop. The water began to rise. I couldn't move the boat; the water kept rising toward the rock above my head. We were crushed and drowned. The lesson? Clueless, I imagined it was the origin of my fear of breathing in the water and failing swimming tests five times in my present life.

"Let's go to a happy life." Tracy counted me down, down, down, deeper down, until I was at one.

"Are you inside or outside? Are you alone or with some-one?"

"I'm in a bistro with long communal tables covered with red and white checked tablecloths."

"Are you male or female?"

"I'm a male singer in his forties; I have dark hair. I'm singing for the crowd. Everyone is happy. We're friends. I have no partner, but everyone loves me."

"What is the lesson in this life?"

"People can be happy without partners."

Tracy counted me back to "waking life" and asked, "How was this for you?"

"It was interesting, but I still don't know the lessons I learned. The images and lifetimes were very vivid, but I don't think they answered my initial question about my marriage."

"The problems you have in this life are due to a faulty belief system." I was puzzled but didn't ask what she meant, fearing I would frustrate her. I waited to learn about faulty belief systems until I attended the ThetaHealing Technique School, years and years later.

two

Monte and the Dream Group

Humpty Dumpty Marriage

A few weeks before our wedding, my intuition told me to call it off, but I didn't listen. As I had feared, my marriage was fraught with problems from the beginning. Throughout the fourteen years, the marriage whipped from fear to hope and back with attempts to anchor it through couple's therapy. Finally, he left—for another woman. Impotent rage and despair eviscerated me.

I continued to see the therapist alone. One day he told me there was no prospect of putting the marriage back together again. No hope. It was over. No going back for repairs.

"Why can't we have one last conversation?" I was confounded.

"He doesn't have the skills," the therapist said.

I left the therapist's office sobbing uncontrollably and sat down on a bench in the hallway to gain enough control to drive home. *He doesn't have the skills? Did he say, "He doesn't have the skills"? How can that be? Can't we have a good-bye conversation at the very least?* The therapist passed me in the hallway on his way out the main door. I was on my own.

Over the next several months, I continued in therapy. Before one of those sessions, I had a vivid dream. My therapist did not discuss it but referred me instead to a dream group leader, Claire Limmer. I had nothing to lose, so I called her.

"I no longer conduct dream groups," she told me, and my heart sank. "But I think Montague Ullman does."

I had never heard of Montague Ullman, but gathering up my courage, I called. He gave me directions to his home, where he conducted a dream group on Monday evenings.

The Dream Group

The following Monday evening, I drove to Monte's home in Ardsley, New York. I didn't know what to expect, but curious, I looked forward to it. He welcomed me, and I took a seat in his cozy living room. His wife's baby grand piano was in one corner; his books lined two walls. His daughter's intricate cityscape collage was a prominent feature on the wall next to the hallway.

Because I was a newcomer, I listened and followed the "rules" of his structured approach. All the participants were intelligent, caring, and reflective individuals. As was my custom, I had more confidence when I didn't realize what I was getting into, so I eagerly participated. Clearly it took courage to share a dream, bare one's soul, publicize those unedited images and plots not always complimentary to one's public face. Monte was a strong, compassionate leader who allowed the dreamer to explore only as far as he wished, which is essential to building trust and safety.

Little did I know that I would go to Monte's dream group for the next fifteen years, excluding a few sabbaticals. When I rejoined after one of my sabbaticals, the group met on Saturday mornings. The members had changed. One woman left her home at eight o'clock every Saturday morning to come to the group, a two-hour round trip. Another woman, a mother whose son had died on the football field of a local high school, struggled for support unavailable from her husband.

As I helped process more and more dreams, I realized I learned as much from the dreams of others as from my own.

I even took a couple of Monte's seminars to teach how to lead Ullman dream groups. He was adamant that even a person without mental health credentials could lead dream groups if the person followed his method, but I had no intention of leading dream groups, as I felt inadequate.

Over time, various members joined and left the group. But four of us continued together for well over ten years. Two women, each a licensed clinical social worker, had private practices. They offered many in-depth insights. One woman, a PhD in English literature, often mentioned characters and archetypes to illustrate her points. An insightful and intelligent male English professor at a community college frequently discussed his own book with Monte. I felt out of my league. Although I possessed a healthy background in psychology from my special education preparation, I had no Jungian analytical training. Nevertheless, I told myself, "Dreams are dreams, no matter who you are. They are real social and intellectual equalizers." I took a deep breath and kept participating, and along the way, Monte encouraged and patiently trained everyone.

After a few years, I realized that I knew my dream group confidants on a very different level from most colleagues. As a teacher, I was familiar with coworkers' families, their personalities, and where they lived and traveled. I knew none of this information about my dream colleagues, sometimes not even their last names. Instead I perceived their inner struggles, which often referred to personal problems. My relationship with dream sharers was more intimate than it was with my work colleagues. Of course, all dream group information is confidential; members promised it would never leave the room. The compassion and inspiration of the group enabled members to alter their life paths in positive ways.

Each of those Saturdays, the group processed two dreams. Ordinarily the first person used an hour and forty-five minutes; the second person had less time, depending on how much time we spent at the break. Either Janet, Monte's wife, baked something, or Monte went to the local bakery earlier in the morning to get scrumptious pastries. He had a generous, compassionate heart. The breaks allowed time for stories about his research and younger life.

So that is how I came to dream work. You can read more about the specific Ullman Dream Group Process in *Dream Digging Guide 1* and in Appendix A.

three

Why Do We Dream?

Why do we dream? What is the brain doing while we sleep? To help answer these questions, let's look at how our brain waves vary over twenty-four hours with our activities.

What Is the Brain Doing When We Are Awake?

Brain waves (gamma, beta, alpha, theta, and delta) can be measured by an electroencephalogram (EEG), a report from data gathered by a special cap with electrodes that sends signals to a computer that records brain wave patterns. Let's follow Ernie, a professor, through a typical day to see how his brain waves change with his activities. He is a medical doctor who conducts research and instructs medical students at a large university.

11:00 A.M.

Ernie is in the classroom lecturing medical students. Because he's alert, focused, and confident in his preparation and delivery, he is predominately in a beta brain wave. Following is an example of one second of a beta brain wave on an EEG:

BETA
16 - 30 Hz

Alertness
Concentration
Cognition

Beta waves range between 16 and 30 hertz. When a student asks a question, Ernie's brain wave is closer to 30 hertz.

12:30 P.M.

After class, Ernie goes to his lab. He and his assistants are working on a complicated problem, so now Ernie's brain waves may cycle faster into the gamma range:

GAMMA
31 - 100 Hz

Insight
Peak focus
Expanded
consciousness

While talking, he is in the beta range; while he is thinking and "grasping" a new concept, gamma waves register. Brain waves typically fluctuate between states during one activity.

4:00 P.M.

Toward the end of his day, Ernie is tired and looking forward to a Reiki treatment. As he lies prone on the table, the practitioner puts his hands just above Ernie's back. The practitioner is relaxed; Ernie is feeling more relaxed—now they are both in an alpha brain wave, an altered state with a focused attention, a state of light hypnosis. Their brain waves are slowed. As the problems of the day drift into his mind, Ernie visualizes a partial solution. The energy from the Reiki practitioner's hands is

ALPHA
8 - 15 Hz

Relaxation
Visualization
Creativity

warm and invigorating. As Ernie visualizes white energy entering his sometimes painful shoulder, the pain decreases:

What Is the Brain Doing When We Are Asleep?

10:30 P.M.

It's been a long day. Ernie relaxes in his bed, prepared for sleep and about to drift off. He enters stage 1 of sleep—not quite sleeping, not quite awake. Knowing that dreams sometimes help solve problems, he sets the intention to have a dream to help him take the next step in his lab. His eyes are still open as he drifts from a beta to alpha and into the theta brain wave state. In this transition between sleep and wakefulness, Ernie could be easily awakened and return to the beta brain wave state, but now his EEG indicates he is in a theta brain wave. This deeply relaxed, semihypnotic state enables him to feel deep, raw emotions; improve his creativity; and sleep restfully. In the theta brain wave, he creates the content of his dreams. As he drifts off, he remembers fragments of conversations of the day. An image of riding his tricycle down the street as a three-year-old pops into his mind.

As he slips into stage 2 of sleep, his eye movements stop, heart rate slows, and body temperature decreases. The brain begins to produce sleep spindles, bursts of activity that last for a half second. His EEG indicates that he remains in a theta brain wave characteristic of both stage 1 and stage 2 of sleep:

THETA
4 - 7 Hz

Meditation
Intuition
Memory

11:30 P.M.

Ernie now enters stages 3 and 4 of sleep, a delta brain wave. He is totally relaxed in a deep sleep, in a delta wave state that sometimes fluctuates into a theta brain wave:

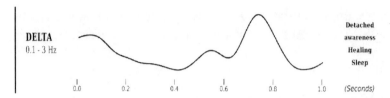

In stage 4, the deepest sleep, Ernie has difficulty awakening. If forced to awaken in stage 4, Ernie will be groggy and disoriented. Bedwetting, night terrors, and sleepwalking can occur in stage 4—but not for Ernie. During the last hour, Ernie has gone from being awake in a beta brain wave to deep sleep in a delta brain wave. There is no dreaming—yet (Hillman 2014).

12:30–1:30 A.M.

Ernie's eyes appear to flutter under his closed eyelids. Now Ernie is entering a rapid eye movement (REM) phase of sleep, when dreaming typically occurs. His EEG registers alpha brain waves. During the next hours, Ernie goes through this cycle five times. He has four or five dreams that night, but Ernie only remembers the last dream he had before he awakens. Dreams typically vaporize if they aren't recorded immediately when they end.

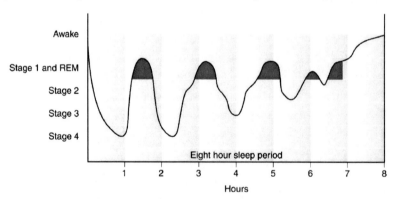

What Happens during REM Sleep?

During the REM phase of sleep, the eye movements, EEG patterns, and heart and breathing rates are similar to those while awake. The first period of REM typically lasts ten minutes. Each successive REM stage gets longer, and the final one may last up to an hour. About 20 to 25 percent of an adult's total sleep is in REM, when dreaming occurs. Some dreams can occur in non-REM phases, but most dreams, especially the ones remembered, occur during REM sleep (Susmakova 2004).

Are There Benefits to Dreaming?

According to Susmakova (2004), the scientific community generally accepts the following functions of sleep:

- conservation of energy
- restoration of tissues and growth
- regulation of body temperature (sleep-deprived rats have a temperature increase of approximately 10 degrees; sleep decreases temperature)
- regulation of emotions (in sleep-deprived humans, concentration and goal interest are decreased; therefore, scientists suspect that non-REM sleep helps to regulate some emotions)
- support for neural development (prenatal six-month-olds spend 80 percent of their time in REM sleep, whereas adults spend 25 percent of sleep time in the REM phase)
- consolidation of memory and learning during REM and non-REM sleep, as evidenced by a transfer between the cortex and hippocampus

The field of psychology proposes that sleep and dreaming offer more than physical benefits. Some practitioners in this field believe that interpretation of dreams provides ideas and solutions. Psychology faculty member of Harvard Medical School Deirdre Barrett (2001) provides many examples of artists, scientists, and athletes who have used dreams for their creations, inventions, and performances. Surrealist painters and filmmakers Salvador Dalí and Luis Buñuel utilized dreams extensively. Ingmar Bergman transferred some of his dreams directly into his films. Author Mary Wollstonecraft Shelley dreamed the basis of *Frankenstein*. Barrett also describes scientists who worked on their inventions and discoveries during the day and became blocked on a detail. In their dreams, they became the observer to a solution: Paul Horowitz, who built control mechanisms for telescopes; Admiral Yi Sun-sin, who built the turtle boat to repel the Japanese naval forces. Gandhi got his idea of passive resistance, the hunger strike, in a dream. In 1844, Elias Howe, struggling with a way to make the sewing machine needle hold a thread, dreamed of a needle with a hole in it. To this day, sewing machine needles have a hole to hold the top thread. Leonid Hambro, Victor Borge's straight man and pianist for WQXR, and Vladimir Horowitz both dreamed the fingerings for their intricate piano performances.

Other dreamers have diagnosed their own illnesses as allopathic medical doctors dismissed their concerns. Wanda Burch (2003), in the habit of recording all her dreams, feared she had breast cancer. Her doctor dismissed her concern time and time again. However, Wanda's dreams provided the courage to insist on further tests. Sure enough, the feelings in the dreams and their interpretation indicated the seriousness of her breast cancer. She continued to apply her dream imagery to augment her healing. She now teaches others how to discover "healing paths and direct lines to the sacred through their dreams" (246). Another cancer survivor, Kathleen O'Keefe-Kanavos (2014, xv), says, "Your inner self uses signs and symbols that include and go beyond dreams to communicate with you, especially during any crisis such as divorce, financial problems, and health issues. No matter how confusing they may seem, your dreams are always telling you something." She now helps others connect with their inner physicians through dreams, meditation, and prayer. Another dream worker, Tallulah Lyons (2012), teaches cancer patients how to find healing imagery in their dreams. Dreams have revealed a wide variety of healing information.

This chapter described the physiology of sleep and dreams and some of their benefits, but what creates the dream images? Where do the images originate? Freud said that dreams are the royal road to the unconscious mind, suggesting that the mind creates dream content. But what is the mind?

four

How Is Dream Content Connected with ThetaHealing?

Many of our dreams are formed during the REM phases of sleep, during theta brain wave activity. But where do dream images originate? What determines the content of our dreams? And how does dreaming relate to the ThetaHealing technique?

As ThetaHealers know, the theta brain wave facilitates their connection to the Creator of All That Is, the Source Energy, the energy of meditation and intuition. The theta brain wave state enables them to connect to the subconscious mind and find and change limiting beliefs, most of which are unknown to our conscious waking minds. So why is the subconscious mind so important? How does it work? The hypnotherapy–ThetaHealing point of view outlines the parts of the mind (Simmerman 2007).

The Mind

The mind exists to keep us safe. It is purposeful and seeks meaning by relating events. It's the software that runs the brain organ, the central processing unit. The psychology field conceptualizes the mind as having parts: the conscious and subconscious minds. Some people acknowledge a third part, the supercon-scious, as the connection to spirit, peace, calmness, uncondi-tional love—something that exists beyond time and space. This universal awareness is accessed through meditation, an altered state.

The Conscious Mind

The conscious mind is aware of our environment and produces thoughts about our perceptions of events. Our senses accept in-formation: we see, hear, feel (tactile), smell, and taste. The con-scious mind looks, listens, and learns. What does it do with this information? It analyzes and criticizes, accepts or rejects based on subconscious mind content. That's all. In contrast, the un-conscious mind runs our lives.

The Unconscious Mind–Subconscious Mind

Hypnotherapy training institutes prefer the term *subconscious* to *unconscious*. For them, *unconscious* means without aware-ness, sensation, or cognition. It has the connotation of being unresponsive or comatose. They prefer the term *subconscious,* with the possibility of accessing its contents. Although the func-tions of the subconscious mind are described separately, note that these functions are intertwined and interdependent.

It controls the autonomic nervous system. The subcon-scious receives sensory input from the conscious mind. On the basis of this information, it automatically regulates heart rate, breathing rate, and the endocrine and digestive systems. For ex-ample, if a person sees an alligator coming at him, he doesn't think, "Time to be afraid." He automatically feels fear; his heart rate and adrenaline production increase so he can run. Another example: we don't consciously think, "Breathe in, breathe out." Breathing is automatic and varies according to emotions, which automatically influence the hormones that enable us to fight, flee, or freeze. The subconscious often interprets our safety dif-ferently from the conscious. The conscious mind is not aware of all our subconscious programs. For example, why do some of us fear water, especially if we have not had any adverse experience with swimming or water? Where do our phobias come from? Because our subconscious programs run us, they often over-rule the logic of the conscious mind. Where do these programs come from?

The subconscious is a memory bank. Each of us perceives events differently. Lipton (2005, 165–66), a cellular biologist, explains,

> The subconscious is an emotionless database of stored pro-grams, whose function is strictly concerned with reading environmental signals and engaging in hard-wired behavioral programs, no questions asked, no judgments made. The sub-conscious mind is a programmable "hard drive" into which our life experiences are downloaded.

These perceptions, stored as memories, contribute to beliefs and programs. The subconscious accumulates our experiences, memories, and valid and invalid beliefs to control our behavior to keep us safe. From a ThetaHealing point of view, our beliefs come from a variety of sources:

- our experiences throughout life: core level
- our ancestors' beliefs that are passed down to us: genetic level
- societal, very old ancestral beliefs and beliefs of unde-termined origin: history level
- soul-level beliefs that permeate our spirits

Lipton relates belief acquisition to brain waves and age. Children aged between birth and two years are in a delta brain wave most of the time. From two to six, they are predominately in a theta brain wave. In the receptive theta and delta states, children accept without question information around them. Their literal interpretations of this information are stored in the subconscious mind. Children before the age of six or seven have no discernment; they have not developed a filter, what hypno-therapists describe as the Critical Factor. This filter, active in people older than seven, helps the conscious mind check with the subconscious programs to determine the validity of incom-ing information. Knowing that all information enters a child's subconscious as literal fact, teachers and parents are warned to monitor their statements to small children. "Stupid. How many times do I have to tell you?" "Stop it! You can't do that." "You'll never amount to anything!" These statements may arise from frustration or an attempt to correct the child's behavior, but to the child, these are truths that become subconscious programs that sabotage future endeavors. Because delta and theta brain wave states provide access to the subconscious, ThetaHealers guide their clients into these brain wave states to help them find and change unwanted beliefs.

The subconscious is the seat of our emotions. To keep our bodies safe, the subconscious controls our emotions. For example, adults have learned that when they face a loaded gun, they should become afraid. This fear generates a series of physiological responses, such as a rush of adrenalin, which increases breathing and heart rates and puts muscles on high alert, ready to fight, flee, or freeze. For a short time, massive amounts of peptides help resolve a danger by flooding our muscles with energy to flee or to perform extraordinary feats to escape danger. During this time, energy does not go to our stomachs or internal organs. The feeling of butterflies in the stomach or vomiting is evidence of this. After the crisis resolves, and the person feels safe once again, the hormonal system rebalances (homeostasis), and energy returns to internal organs and supports the immune system.

If the danger does not resolve soon, the body continues in this state of high alert, producing stress. Lipton (2005, 152) agrees, summarizing many researchers: "almost every major illness that people acquire has been linked to chronic stress." Pert (1999) explains from a chemical point of view that a continual state of alertness produces continual neuropeptides, which suppress the immune system and allow many diseases and adverse physical conditions to flourish. Lipton (2016) explains from a cellular point of view, contrasting a protective mode with a growth mode, that stress precipitates hormones to fight or flee, which puts the body in a protective mode. If the body continues in this protective mode, all resources are allocated to protection.

Resources are unavailable for growth to regenerate cells to heal wounds or fight infection. A protective mode leaves the immune system impeded, unable to inhibit disease. During times of stress, the immune system is not a priority.

As described, emotions fuel our hormones. In addition, emotions provide the foundation for beliefs. Emotions are triggered by events and perceptions, whether we want them to be or not. For example, a first-grade child, Tommy, is experiencing difficulty learning to read. The teacher becomes frustrated and says, "You're hopeless. You'll never learn to read." Those statements, followed by taunts from classmates, cause Tommy embarrassment and shame. His system goes into protective mode. His stomach muscles contract, causing nausea. Now reading is associated with nausea. To avoid this pain, he goes to the nurse during reading class, which puts him further behind. His subconscious mind stayed alert and created the belief that "reading is painful. It makes me sick. I can't read. Better avoid it." Daniel Siegel (2011) describes the interaction between Tommy's mind and the brain: "What fires together, wires together." For example, if the mind perceives an emotion (fear) during a specific firing of neurons (reading), then when that pattern fires again (reading), the person experiences that emotion (fear).

Both the brain and the subconscious maintain this association, now a program. Even at age forty, Tommy avoids reading. When his conscious mind sees print, his subconscious says, "Oh, you're in for nausea. You can't read." No wonder he avoids going to restaurants, which requires reading a menu, although he may not consciously be aware that his belief of "reading is painful" is the root cause.

The subconscious is the seat of creativity. The subconscious creates some of our dreams. It also helps to solve problems and create solutions. Have you ever faced a conundrum, feeling totally blocked, and said, "I'll sleep on it" or "I'll put it on the shelf for now"? Napping or sleeping shuts off the conscious mind's interfering chatter and allows the subconscious to do its creative work. Often a solution becomes evident after a night's sleep or a short nap or just a day of thinking about other things. Sometimes the solution comes in a vivid dream. Even if you don't remember dreaming, you may realize a solution upon awakening. It's a gut feeling, an intuition, not to be questioned. Most of us are conditioned to ignore our intuition because, once again, the conscious mind interferes with "logic." How many times have we regretted ignoring our intuition: "if only I had listened to my gut."

Dream Images

What creates the content of dreams? According to Ullman (1996, 2), dream images are metaphors for our waking life: "the images of our dreams turn out to be metaphorically crafted references to feelings and concerns that surface while we are asleep. . . . Asleep and dreaming, we are, in effect, manufacturing potential visual metaphors of a very personal and interesting kind."

Burch (2003, xv), a cancer survivor, states more graphically,

> I am alive because I dream. Dreams come from deep within our souls, drawn from a vast repository of memory deeper than we access in our daily lives. Dreams are given to us in the context of our individual life experience; some dreams recall our simple past, and some evoke a more complex past that stirs haunting memories of places and people no longer familiar to us. Some dreams play out scenes from our busy lives, solve simple daily problems, or play back a moment of pleasure. Some dreams pull forth the secret wishes of our heart or predict events a day, a year, or a decade in the future. Other dreams, perhaps the most important ones, warn us of death and illness—and many of those dreams present paths for healing.

If dreams come from the subconscious mind, a memory bank that holds beliefs and programs, why wouldn't dream images involve subconscious beliefs? If the subconscious programs promote or destroy health, and if dreams are metaphors of events of our lives, why couldn't dream metaphors reveal our subconscious programs and beliefs? If the purpose of dreams is healing, then dream images can help find limiting beliefs that the dreamer can decide to keep or change. Dream work provides a rich resource for the ThetaHealing belief and digging work.

Dreams and ThetaHealing

Dreaming and the ThetaHealing technique share these commonalities:

- Both employ the theta brain wave.
- Both address memories of recent and past events.
- Both address physical issues. Some dreams are metaphors for physical conditions. The ThetaHealing technique teaches how to do body scans to find physical conditions.
- Both address the future. Some dreams are precognitive. Many dreams are unbound by Earth's time and space. ThetaHealing technique teaches how to "remember" the future.
- Both can address beliefs. Dream metaphors can reveal hidden subconscious beliefs. The ThetaHealing technique facilitates finding and changing limiting beliefs.

ThetaHealing work and dream work complement each other. Consider Susan, who dreamed she was carrying a handbag containing rotten meat. Her dream group shared their projections about this image. One group member said, "In my imagined version of this dream, I fear there is something wrong with my stomach or my bowels. Something's rotten there." For this dream group participant, rotten meat in a handbag was a metaphor for a "rotten" or diseased internal organ, a metaphor produced in Susan's dreaming theta brain wave state to reflect her physical condition. Susan's subconscious was warning her to get medical help.

Dreams and ThetaHealing share similar concepts of the future. Many dreams seem to be outside of time and space, perhaps accessing the Universal Energy, Universal Awareness, Spirit, Source Energy, or superconscious. Sometimes dream images from the distant past are mixed with recent waking life events or future events. Before the 9/11 terrorist attack in

America, diverse people reported having had dreams of explosions, flames, and buildings coming down (Wagner 2015). Dreamers did not know at the time of the dream that these were predictions. Some guests of Osama bin Laden had dreams of pilots playing soccer with Americans. Another guest reported a dream of carrying a plane. Bin Laden ordered these men not to tell anybody their dreams about an airplane, fearing that that his planned attack would be revealed before it was carried out (Boxer 2001). Again, there is a similarity with the ThetaHealing technique. To predict the future, ThetaHealers go into a theta brain wave state—the same as a dreaming state—connect to the Creator, and command to remember "the last time I . . . ," inserting a future event. For example, wanting to know if my next plane will be delayed, the command is, "Show me the last time I flew from London to Denver. Are the flights on time?" In both dreaming and ThetaHealing, there is no time and space as we know it in waking life on Earth.

The Role of Energy

ThetaHealers access the energy of the Creator to heal physical bodies, change beliefs, and perform many tasks. Our beliefs and emotions, based on how we perceive information, are energy and require energy to be maintained:

> Information and energy go hand-in-hand. For example, when we learn our best friend has died (information) we feel sad (energy). We have learned to interpret this information as bringing sadness. We base our subsequent actions on this information and energy; we seek comfort from other friends. (Siegel 2011, 52–53)

Lipton (2016) has emphasized the role of energy in our lives starting at the cellular level. In the early 1970s, his research found that our genes no longer are the sole determiners of our characteristics. Rather, the environment of the cell, the blood, sends signals to the cell nucleus, which is 50 percent DNA and 50 percent protein. The protein receives the environmental signals from the blood, changes shape, and sends signals to the DNA to make an RNA copy. Sometimes the RNA copy is changed (methylated) abnormally, contributing to disease. Our skin is another gatherer of environmental signals. Skin cell receptors detect temperature and texture, for example. The signals are sent to the brain, which creates a picture in our minds. Based on this picture, the brain sends chemicals to various organs and muscles to cause movement, digestion, sneezing, scratching, or whatever the subconscious and conscious minds determine to keep us safe. DNA might hold the "recipe," but environmental energy activates or "makes the recipe." Lipton also describes how beliefs and programs were transmitted to our cells as we were developing in the womb. We didn't choose them; they were simply downloaded. All these examples depend on energy to activate body chemistry, which controls our lives—with or without our permission.

ThetaHealers have learned these principles. Biology now explains how this works. Beliefs are transmitted through energy—beliefs we have inherited from parents and ancestors for many generations and learned through repetition. "Whatever is said to us, through us, and by us, for thirty consecutive days, becomes a subconscious habit, with or without our permission" (Otto n.d.). The most important work of a ThetaHealer is to activate the Creator's energy and to find and change limiting beliefs so our bodies and minds can heal.

From Lipton's research, we draw several conclusions:

- Emotions are energy.
- Thoughts are energy.
- Beliefs are energy or require energy.
- DNA requires energy for expression.

The ThetaHealing Technique employs energy to help heal all of the above.

Let's find out how dreams can reveal hidden beliefs—but first you must remember your dreams.

five

⁓

Recall and Record Your Dreams

Recall Your Dreams

The first step of Dream Digging is to recall your dream. Dreams typically vaporize when we try to capture them with words or images. Because dreams originate in the subconscious mind, our "incorruptible core," as Monte would say, they tell the truth about us, the truth our waking minds would prefer not to know, much less acknowledge in public. That's why dreams tend to evaporate when we attempt to capture them with words. In addition, most dream language is imagery, so we are translating images to words, a challenge for all of us. If you want to recall dreams but say "I don't remember my dreams," consider the following suggestions.

Sleep Habits

1. Go to bed at approximately the same time every night.
2. Get between seven and nine hours of sleep each night. You need to get REM phases of sleep to dream. REM cycles occur about every ninety minutes, and the most vivid dreams usually occur during the last hour of

sleep. If you only get six or fewer hours of sleep, you will probably dream much less frequently.

3. Create a restful environment without TV, Internet, and e-mail devices. Eliminate noise and light if you have difficulty falling asleep.

4. Don't eat or drink alcohol before bed. Some medications may interfere with sleep.

5. If you can avoid using an alarm clock, do so. Put your lights on a timer or have someone silently and gently wake you.

6. Calm your mind before drifting off to sleep. Meditation may be helpful.

7. Put a pen and paper next to your bed to record your dream. If you use a notebook, open it to a blank page so you don't have to look for a page upon awakening.

Be Careful What You Think as You Drift Off to Sleep

1. Remember, whatever you are thinking as you drift to sleep plays all night long. This includes worries, targets of anger, and things you are grateful for.

2. Set the intention to recall your dreams. Say to yourself, "I recall my dreams." If you fear your dreams or don't want to remember them, recall is challenging.

3. If you wish, ask for a dream that . . . (creates something, solves a problem, teaches you something).

4. Enter a meditative state, imagining a wave of relaxation slowly moving from the top of your head, through your body, and out through the tips of your toes—and drift off to sleep. Imagine that wave of relaxation going through each muscle group.

Record Your Dream

1. Wake up slowly. Before you get out of bed and while still groggy, *write what you remember* of the dream.

2. Record your *feelings while dreaming* (not the feelings you have about the dream). If you don't recall feelings or have difficulty getting in touch with your feelings, ask yourself, "If I had to choose one of the basic

feelings—mad, sad, glad, or afraid—which would I choose?" Often nuances of one of the basic feelings will appear.

3. *Write down as many details as possible.* Sometimes drawing images aids recall.

4. *Do not revise or change spelling.* Misspellings can be very important in finding the messages.

5. Put the *date* at the top of the page.

6. Put a few notes about *events and concerns of the day(s) before the dream.* This can be done after you get out of bed, but don't forget to do it. This information will help you recall the context, the contributing factors, of the dream.

The template in Appendix B contains the categories for your dream journal.

Other Considerations

An audio recording of your dream (on your phone, for example) may allow you to capture the dream more easily, but at the expense of missing the puns, homophones, and misspellings that are important.

The next chapter describes how a dream group helped me decide to make a life change.

six

~)(~

My Orphan Dream

As I took part in Monte's dream group, I experienced personal understanding and healing and observed these in dream group participants. Trust increased; I recounted more dreams. I was grateful for the compassionate members who took turns baring their souls. Then, one Friday night, I had *My Orphan Dream.*

Agitated, I awoke at odds with myself. "What brought this dream? What in the world does it mean?" Since the dream group met that morning, I swallowed breakfast and got in my car.

"Should I skip the dream group?" I mulled over the dream during the twenty-minute trip. It was disgusting. I hated to reveal thoughts and fears yet unknown to me, but this dream was important—I just knew it. Near tears as I turned off the parkway, I convinced myself to endure the pain for a morning. "Perhaps someone else will bring a dream so important that it will preempt mine." I wanted to work on mine, but I dreaded the pain.

As I parked in front of Monte's home, I recognized the cars: Doris, a psychotherapist; Jane, a clinical social worker in private practice; Eddy, an intellectual college professor. Marie might come, too. We had solidified into a long-term, trusting group.

I entered the room and noted Monte in his customary seat. A newcomer was present. I greeted everyone and claimed my habitual seat on the couch. Funny how each member had his "own" seat every other week. A newcomer was the only person who usurped another's seat, but not mine this time. Monte introduced George, the guest who wanted to experience the dream group.

"Does anyone have a short, recent dream to share?" Monte inquired. A long pause. Silence.

"I have one," I mumbled.

Because no one else volunteered, Monte asked, "When did you have the dream?"

"Friday night. Last night."

"Tell us your dream slowly so we can write it verbatim . . . and speak loudly!" My voice is soft and difficult for anyone to hear, let alone Monte with his hearing aids. He was always telling me to speak up. I took a deep breath.

> *I encountered an orphan,*
> *Dirty, starving.*
> *He had chewed his own fingers.*
> *He didn't seem to be in pain.*
> *He had no pants.*
> *There was a stack of used clothing;*
> *I thought I could find some pants in the stack.*
> *There was one pair, a maroon, knit pair of sweat pants.*
> *I didn't know if he would like it. [sic]*
> *There was a green pair, but full of burned holes.*

"The next step," Monte explained to George, "is to clarify who and what are real in waking life. Sometimes we ask ages of people, relationships between people, and if colors appeared in the dream." Monte turned to me. "Tell us what or who is real in waking life."

I felt I was the orphan but left this unsaid. "No one is real in waking life. The boy's hair was a matted and filthy mess. The place was outside, in a homeless atmosphere, maybe under a bridge. I don't know this place in waking life."

"Were there any feelings in the dream?" Monte asked. Turning to George, he said, "We want to know what Janet felt in the dream, not what she felt after awakening."

I responded, near tears, "Hopelessness." The weight of the dream permeated the room.

Monte proceeded to the next step of turning the dream over to the group. "In this step the group members, without looking at the dreamer, pretend that the dream is their own and give feelings using the stem, 'If it were my dream . . .' or 'In my dream . . .' They are our projections which the dreamer is free to accept or reject. They allow the dreamer to expand her own emotions and symbol interpretation as she chooses. We are not interpreting the dream for her. That's why we speak without looking at the dreamer." I listened and wrote the comments in my journal to ponder in the coming weeks.

"Let's start with feelings," said Monte.

I listened to their projections:

- In my dream, I am frightened.
- I am sleepwalking but awake.
- I have been unconscious, completely unaware.
- I am inadequate. I need to understand what I can do.
- Deep inside I want to take care of the child. I want or need to nurture myself.
- Maybe I can help. I am somewhat competent.
- I find burn holes, another horror. It's just one horror after another.
- I hesitate to take care of something.
- I fear not knowing, and I must quiet that fear.
- I lack responsiveness to pain. I just accept it.
- The boy, hurt so long, is in shock.
- The child has no one. He is abandoned and alone.
- The only nourishment is eating oneself as a feral animal.
- I am beyond contact, so I can't just put on pants.
- I disassociate. To satisfy my needs, I choose the way that gets me least emotionally involved.

The contributions had become repetitive, so Monte asked the group to play with metaphors and symbols:

- "Maroon—I am marooned on a desert island."
- "Maroon and green make a bizarre Christmas."
- "Green symbolizes hope, but this green has been devastated."
- "This dream depicts Bosch's hell: a voracious person eating fingers, blood, sweat, and burning."
- "I identify with the child. In my dream I am helpless and abandoned. I can't grow up without fingers."
- "In my dream he feels bereft."
- "This dream is a metaphor for the life of an abandoned, dependent human (self)."
- "I must look elsewhere, not in a stack of used clothing."
- "Sad children suck on fingers to soothe themselves, but this one must eat himself alive."
- "No pants leaves one vulnerable."
- "Having no pants is a greater abuse not to be mentioned."
- "In my dream I am sexless and most vulnerable."
- "My sexual side is exposed; I want to cover it."

When the group finished with metaphors, Monte said, "Let's go to the next step of returning the dream to the dreamer." He looked at me and said, "Do you want to continue?"

"Yes."

"Say whatever you want. We will not interrupt you. Take as long as you wish; just tell us when you are finished." Monte explained to George, "Asking the dreamer to state when she is finished allows her time to pause and think."

I took a deep breath. Their responses reminded me of my work situation. Then, with tears in my eyes, I began, "I have no support from my superiors at work. My role is to support others, but I receive no support. The job is eating me alive, just as the orphan is eating his own fingers.

"Someone said, 'My sexual side is exposed. There are no pants.' The men have closed ranks, which leaves no way for me to join the team. They wear the pants; I have no pants. Women administrators don't count in my school district.

"Another person said, 'I have to look elsewhere, not in a stack of used clothing.' I have to face the fact that nothing will change in terms of support for me. Any support for me at work has the quality of used clothing with burned holes, a castoff. I am a castoff at work . . . that is all I can say."

To George, Monte stated, "The next step is to explore the context of the dream since events in the dreamer's life create metaphors, symbols, and puns. Because the dreamer is in control, before each step, we ask if she wants to proceed."

Monte looked at me and asked, "Do you want to continue?" I nodded, knowing I had a choice. "Your dream was Saturday morning. Are there any events that took place on Friday that might be relevant and you want to share?"

"On Friday night I was thinking what happened Thursday. I felt the superintendent and business administrator had been deceptive, so I made an appointment for 10:00 A.M. to discuss the matter. The superintendent promised me plenty of time to explain my position. When I arrived at 10:00, I learned he had moved the meeting to 3:30 P.M. When I arrived at 3:30, the good ol' boys had arrived earlier and finished the discussion. I had no opportunity to state my position.

"It's been four long years of massive change in education. I am in charge of K–12 curricula revision to meet state standards and exam requirements. This requires managing people who prefer not to change. I do have support at the department chair level, but change threatens principals, who are on constant guard to keep their power and control of staff and money. After four years, the undercutting, manipulation, and back stabbing are more than I can endure. My habit of saying things as I see them gets me in trouble sometimes. I refuse to join with the manipulators, those who are cheating the system. I want to retire, but if I stay another year, my pension will increase. I am scared and uncertain . . . that's all I can say."

"Do you want to continue to the next step?" Monte asked. I nodded. Monte explained to George, "Now is time for the playback. Someone reads the dream aloud to the dreamer, changing 'I' to 'you.' If the dreamer hears the dream again, sometimes more insights and connections come to mind. Group members can ask questions regarding specific images to gain more information."

As I listened to the dream read scene by scene, I attempted to recall other events. I shared examples of being left out of discussions and undercut during the budget process. I was the only woman administrator in the central office. "Knowledge is power, and if they keep knowledge from me, they hold on to power, a strategy used by power seekers in the corporate world. I simply cannot get on the team."

Monte asked, "Do you want to continue to the Orchestration?"

"Yes, of course."

Monte explained to George, "The Orchestration step allows the group members to offer new connections which the dreamer has not stated. These comments must be based on what the dreamer has shared but not yet connected to an idea or feeling. No advice or empathetic statements are appropriate. These are still the group member's projections, which the dreamer can accept or ignore as she chooses."

I noted their ideas:

- "Job and money don't make a life. Sometimes we have to stop doing life's work for physical and psychological survival."
- "The terror is you have no support, no husband."
- "For me, this dream holds confusion and conflict. Should I follow 'the grass is always greener' at the expense of eating myself and the terror of being on my own?"
- "The first need is pants. In my dream I must leap over unhappiness and take care of my basic needs first. My immediate needs are neglected."
- "It's destructive both at work and for inner needs, a real conundrum."
- "That image of no pants on an orphan asks, 'Who wears the pants in this family?' For me, I need to assume power."
- "I have a tendency to cover the shame of no pants instead of sensing the pain of the orphan, the most impor-

tant thing. I must be aware of my emotions and release shame."
- "If I had cancer that was treatable, would I wait a year to treat it?"

I was numb. "If I had cancer that was treatable, would I wait a year to treat it? Would I wait a year to treat it?" The last statement became a tape loop. I mumbled, "Thank you for your ideas. You gave me a lot to think about." Overwhelmed, I departed. I would have to take time to think about this.

And contemplate I did. I had to do something; my work was eating me alive. I had tried everything to compromise while attempting to fulfill my responsibilities. There was nothing more I could give. "Money isn't everything. I will manage with less money in my pension to preserve my dignity and integrity. I will not let work eat me alive."

At the beginning of the next session, the dreamer who shared during the previous session is asked for any other thoughts that may have occurred in the interim. When asked two weeks later, I responded, "This dream moved me toward retirement. It told me I can no longer neglect myself at the expense of my dignity and self-respect. The image of eating my own fingers as a metaphor for the job is so powerful that I can't ignore it; I have to act. Recalling that image will allay any future doubts. Thank you so much for helping me to move forward."

By the first of June, I had signed the papers to retire. As it turned out, a few months later, the state offered a retirement incentive, so I did not diminish my pension by retiring early. This taught me that money is not the highest priority and that it doesn't pay to agonize about the future. I had enough money to live.

I continued with the dream group. More and more, I realized that just being a group member can precipitate life changes. One morning, the group spent nearly two hours on a long emotional dream. At the end, the dreamer stated, "I don't know why this dream makes me so uncontrollably sad. My career and marriage are going well; my kids are okay."

Monte responded, "A past life regression might be helpful. This sadness might be ancestor related." This comment, intended for someone else, triggered my memory of the past life regression I had had with Tracy years earlier. The images of those past lives were seared into my mind. I'd forgotten how fascinated I'd been with learning hypnosis, but now I could not stop thinking about it. It propelled me to consider learning hypnotherapy.

That summer, I enrolled in the Hypnotherapy Academy of America, then in Santa Fe, for five weeks, and again for two weeks in autumn. Remember that loud noise I constantly heard as a child described in the first chapter? I learned during the natal regression training that I entered this life after being an eight-year-old Jewish boy during the Nazi era. Bulldozers pushed me into a hole as I pretended to be dead. No wonder I had recurring dreams of holes and heard loud noises during the day.

After I completed that training, I started a consulting medical support hypnosis practice in New York City. I attracted a few clients. Although effective, the hypnosis techniques were time consuming. One of my hypnotherapist colleagues searched for an effective practice that worked faster and found the ThetaHealing technique. A year later, off we went to the ThetaHealing Institute of Knowledge to learn about belief work.

seven

The Birth of Dream Digging

The ThetaHealing Technique

Because I was concerned about being labeled "woo-woo" or worse, I wanted to read as many scientific reports about the ThetaHealing technique and hypnosis as I could. I already knew that energy healing modalities had existed for thousands of years and that modern-day Reiki, healing touch, guided imagery, and the ThetaHealing technique probably emerged from these ancient practices because they all share some characteristics:

- altered states of mind
- deep relaxation with a focused attention or consciousness
- a connection to emotions
- a connection to God, the Creative Energy, the Higher Power, the Source, or the Quantum Force

Today we meditate to connect to a Higher Power. And, though others consider it prayer, scientists look to quantum physics for explanations. Gregg Braden (2007, 79) applies physics to the role of human consciousness as we access this quantum force:

It's our ability to purposefully create the conditions of consciousness (thoughts, feelings, emotions and beliefs) that lock one possibility of our choosing into the reality of our lives. Both science and mysticism describe a force that connects everything together and gives us the power to influence how matter behaves—and reality itself—simply through the way we perceive the world around us.

Braden continues to describe the benefits of connecting with the quantum force:

> Through the power of our forgotten inner technology, we can change our bodies and the world. We can heal, bi-locate, be everywhere at once, remote-view, connect telepathically, choose peace and do everything in between. It's all about our power to focus consciousness, which is the great secret of some of our most ancient and cherished traditions. (80)

This perfectly describes the scientific foundation for the ThetaHealing technique. The technique's founder, Vianna Stibal (2014), describes it:

> The ThetaHealing meditation technique was created by Vianna Stibal in 1995 during her own personal journey back to health. Her original book details her personal healing journey and her connection to the Creator utilizing her meditation technique. She did not start teaching the ThetaHealing technique until 2006 or so, after she had perfected the technique on herself.
>
> The ThetaHealing technique is a meditation technique utilizing a spiritual philosophy with the purpose of improvement in mind, body and spirit while getting closer to the Creator of All That Is (our God has many names and we call him Creator). It is a focused prayer to the Creator and allows you to train your mind, body and spirit to clear limiting beliefs and live life with positive thoughts, developing virtues in all that we do. Through meditation and prayer, the ThetaHealing technique creates a positive lifestyle.
>
> The ThetaHealing technique is always taught to be used in conjunction with conventional medicine. It teaches how to put to use one's own natural intuition, relying upon unconditional love of Creator of All That Is to do the actual "work." We believe by focused prayer utilizing a "Theta" and "delta" brainwave

(incorporating physics and quantum physics), you can actually witness the Creator of All That Is create instantaneous physical and emotional well-being. We have learned that through the ThetaHealing technique intuitive abilities can be used to bring about spontaneous changes and physical and emotional well-being.

A crucial feature of the ThetaHealing technique is digging work: a method to find and replace limiting beliefs that block healing and allow disease. Stibal states,

> With growing scientific evidence that toxic emotion can contribute to disease, and the awareness that emotions, feelings, and the power of thought have a direct bearing upon our physical health, there is increasing interest in changing how the mind influences the body to create optimum health. The ThetaHealing technique Belief and Feeling Work empower people with the ability to remove and replace negative emotions, feelings and thoughts with positive, beneficial ones.

Based on these premises, dreams offer another source of finding subconscious beliefs, some of which serve us; others don't.

Sources of Beliefs

Where do beliefs originate?

- Our life experiences instill beliefs.
- Ancestors pass their beliefs and fears to us.
- Society broadcasts beliefs in news and advertising.
- Self-talk reinforces beliefs.

In conversations, we repeat thoughts and ideas, anchoring them in our minds. Remember what hypnotist Robert Otto stated: "Whatever is said to us, through us, or by us for 30 consecutive days becomes a subconscious habit, with or without our permission." Talk and thoughts cement beliefs into our minds.

Marketers certainly know the power of talk and thought. "You deserve a break today—at McDonald's" was the company slogan as early as 1971. McDonald's food is definitely not my favorite, and its jingle is not something I choose to remember, yet it has played in my mind for longer than forty years. How long will children remember that "I'm lovin' it" or "Lovin' beats hatin'" connects them to McDonald's? Multitudes of beliefs from many sources are stuck in our minds, most of which we are unaware.

That's where Dream Digging comes in. Dreams provide windows onto our hidden beliefs. So let's go Dream Digging.

Dream Digging

Perceptions rule our lives. Each of us tells a different story of the same event or person. Your perception of me is not how I perceive myself. I build my public façade based on my self-perceptions. My waking mind edits my words and actions to create what I believe is a socially acceptable identity—all based on my beliefs. We expend enormous amounts of energy to construct and maintain our façades. We hide our perceived faults; we project our perceived attributes. But dreams call our bluff. Dreams provide images from our unedited subconscious minds, thereby exposing our "true" selves, the aspects we don't want to face. The little cartoon character, Triangle, illustrates how a dream can expose beliefs hiding under a façade. A Dream Digging chart found in Appendix C structures the process:

Step 1: Identify the metaphors in the dream.

Step 2: List the characteristics of each metaphor. Describe it: how it looks, smells, sounds, feels.

Step 3: List the emotions of each metaphor. If this is challenging, start with the basic feelings: sad, mad, glad, and afraid. Choose the one that is the most applicable and then find a word that more accurately describes the emotion. It helps to be in a relaxed state, in an alpha or theta brain wave, and just let the feeling bubble up. After all, the dream metaphor came when you were in a theta wave, so let that state help you recall the feeling.

Take a look at Triangle's dream on the next pages.

Triangle hates her sharp points. She wants to be round.

So she creates a shield of roundness.
She buys round clothes and puts on round dark body liner
day after day after day.
She thinks she is beautiful because she looks round.

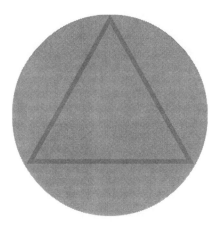

One night Triangle puts down her round shield and has a dream.

Let's see what Triangle has to say about her dream.

"Why was that monster in my dream? I can hardly breathe." Triangle gulped for air. She recorded her dream in her journal. On the Dream Digging chart, she listed the symbols (monster, hatbox, diamond, and stealing the diamond) as well as their physical descriptions. Attaching feelings to the symbols was more challenging. Triangle deliberated with herself:

"What is the monster feeling?"

"Rage, he wants to control and dominate me." She didn't overthink it; without judgment, she wrote what popped into her mind.

"How do I feel about the monster?"

"Scared—no, terrified."

"What is the feeling of the hatbox?"

"Hmm. Safe, protective, or I must protect it. It protects something valuable. I must protect it and hide it."

"What about the diamond?"

"It is precious and beautiful."

"But what are its feelings?"

"It holds love and happiness. It is proud. It is fearful that it will be seen and stolen."

Triangle completed the Feelings column. These descriptions and feelings are unique to Triangle. If you had this dream, the description and feelings of the monster may have been different.

Symbol	Description	Feelings
Monster	Big Green	Rage Wants control Wants to dominate Threatening Terrified of him
Hatbox	White Holds something precious	Safe Must protect it Must hide it
Diamond	Valuable Cut and polished Beautiful Many facets Must not be seen	Love Happy Proud Fear of being seen Fear of being stolen
Action—steal the diamond	Monster will steal the diamond	Fear

Many authorities, Sigmund Freud, Carl Jung, and Fritz Perls, to name a few, consider dream images as parts of the dreamer. All parts of a person have a positive intention, even though the part has outlived its function. Working from this premise, the characteristics and especially the feelings of each dream image apply to the dreamer. Do not skip feelings.

The next step in the Dream Digging process is to make "I" statements for each word in the description and feelings columns. Triangle constructed the following statements:

- I am in a rage.
- I want control.
- I want to dominate. I am domineering.
- I am threatening.
- I am terrified of myself.
- I am safe.
- I must protect myself.
- I must hide.
- I am valuable.
- I am polished.
- I am beautiful.
- I have many facets.
- I must not be seen.
- I am loving.
- I am happy.
- I am proud.
- I fear someone will steal from me—lose myself.
- I must hide what is precious.

"This is nonsense! I don't believe this!" Triangle protested. But muscle testing tells a different story.

Symbol	Description/characteristics	Feelings	"I" statements—beliefs to be verified	Yes/no
Monster	Green Big	Rage Wants control Wants to dominate Threatening Terrified of him	I am in a rage. I want control. I want to dominate. I am domineering. I am threatening. I am terrified of myself.	
Hatbox	White	Holds something precious Safe Must protect it Must hide it	I am safe. I must protect myself. I must hide.	
Diamond	Valuable Cut and polished Beautiful Many facets	Must not be seen Love Happy Proud Fear of being stolen	I am valuable. I am polished. I am beautiful. I have many facets. I must not be seen. I am loving. I am happy. I am proud.	
Action—hide the diamond		Fear Must not be seen	Someone will steal from me. I lose myself. I must hide what is precious.	

eight

$\sim\!\!\!\!\sim\!\!\!\sim$

Muscle Testing

"These beliefs are crazy. I'm not in a rage. Is this stuff really in my mind?" Triangle's thoughts raced.

We are not aware of all the beliefs that are held in our subconscious minds. So muscle testing, although not foolproof, is a method to verify subconscious beliefs.

As Bruce Lipton (2005, 159–60) states, "when your conscious mind has a belief that is in conflict with a formerly learned 'truth' stored in the subconscious mind, the intellectual conflict expresses itself as a weakening of the body's muscles." So if you hold out your arm at shoulder height and state, "My name is [your name]," and someone pushes down on your arm, your arm will stay rigid. However, if you repeat this process stating, "My name is [not your name]," and someone pushes down on your rigid arm, it cannot stay rigid.

For this work, muscle testing only tests our subconscious beliefs, not necessarily the "truth." Muscle testing does not work to determine what vitamins we need, for example. It will tell us what vitamins our subconscious minds believe we need, which may not be the "truth." Now we may indeed need the vitamins our subconscious believes we need, but muscle testing is not the way to establish reliability or validity in this case. With Dream Digging, we want to find what the subconscious mind believes—unbeknownst to the conscious mind. The dreamer must want to know for muscle testing to work. If the dreamer really doesn't want to know, the conscious mind will likely override the subconscious.

How to Muscle Test

Here is another way to muscle test yourself without a person pushing on a rigid arm. Be certain you are well hydrated:

- Stand facing north; take a couple of deep breaths.
- Say, "Yes," and you should rock forward.
- Say, "No," and you should rock backward.
- If you rock in opposite directions, try these techniques:
  - Put your hand facing toward your abdomen, and bring your hand over the top of your head to align your polarity. Do this a few times. There are electrical signals between the brain and muscles all the time. Sometimes electromagnetic devices (computers, cell phones, microwave ovens) interfere as well as causing stress, trauma, and dehydration.
  - Drink some water. The body must be well hydrated to muscle test properly.
- Muscle test again. Say, "My name is [your real name]." You should rock forward.
- Then say, "My name is [someone else's name, not yours]." You should rock backward. Now you are ready to test subconscious beliefs.
- Say, "I am beautiful." Perhaps you think you are beautiful, but your subconscious believes you are not.
- Say, "I deserve plenty of money." Is your subconscious belief different from your conscious belief? Conflicting beliefs prevent you from having plenty of money.

"But Muscle Testing Doesn't Work on Me"

For muscle testing to work, several conditions must be operating:

1. The person must understand and accept that muscle testing indicates what the subconscious believes. It does not indicate the "truth" or opinions of others.

2. It is not effective to find out what foods, vitamins, or treatments you need. It will indicate what foods, vitamins, and treatments your subconscious thinks you need.

3. The person must want to know what the subconscious believes regardless of what the conscious mind wants to project. If a person really does not want to know, muscle testing will not work.

4. If the person is fearful of this information, muscle testing will be unlikely to work. It takes a confident, adventurous spirit.

Now let's check back with Triangle and her potential beliefs.

nine

Subconscious Language to Find Hidden Beliefs

Triangle wants to know what this dream is telling her. She wants to find her subconscious beliefs that are hidden from her conscious mind—and those she would prefer to keep secret.

Triangle has completed the "I" statements in her chart. These statements are unique to the dreamer.

Before muscle testing beliefs, we must be sure that we used the language of the subconscious mind. After all, we wouldn't speak English to a Chinese person who only speaks Chinese.

Subconscious Language

Subconscious language is very literal, similar to the language used when speaking to a five- or six-year-old. It is best for the person testing to say the beliefs in his first language. So imagine speaking to a child in your native tongue. Children as well as the subconscious do ignore negatives. If a child hears "Don't touch the stove," she runs to the stove and touches it. Follow these guidelines when testing subconscious beliefs:

1. Avoid negatives; the subconscious ignores them. When muscle testing a negative statement, put "no" at the end of the sentence: "It is safe to feel my feelings, no." This means it is not safe to feel my feelings. Rocking forward, indicating a "yes," means the statement is true: "It is not safe to feel my feelings." Remember that when you muscle test a statement, a "yes" means that the sentence is true. Another way to state a negative is to use "without." For example, "My life is safe without feeling my feelings."

2. Use literal language: no puns, jokes, metaphors, or double meanings. If someone says, "I need a break," the subconscious interprets "break" literally, and the speaker may experience a broken arm or plate. "Lose weight" propels the subconscious mind to find the weight after it is lost. As a result, the person will lose and regain weight, especially if the person repeats, "I am *losing* weight or I *need to lose* weight." The better statement is "I *release* weight." Note that the word "need" is eliminated because it assumes no action.

3. Speak in the present tense: "I release weight now."

4. Avoid the progressive and future tense: "I am going to clean the house." This action is continually pushed into the future; cleaning will never get done. Instead, use the present tense: "I clean the house now." An exception is stating the goal while using the progressive tense: "I am getting thinner and thinner until I weigh 140" (or the desired weight). This allows the subconscious to release the weight gradually and gives a stopping point. This statement is credible and prevents the monkey mind from saying, "You can't do that. You don't weigh 140 pounds."

5. Avoid "try." "Try" is a contract to fail. If a boss gives an order, and the employee has no intention of fulfilling

it, "I'll try" is a socially acceptable response that hides the intention to ignore the order.

6. Avoid "can." Certainly I can do it, but will I?
7. Avoid "need." "I need to study" is a statement without action.
8. When you catch yourself saying or thinking a negative, say, "Cancel, cancel," so the subconscious can reject the negative thought. Then restate the subject positively.

Our language is extremely important when we want to change our negative patterns. Thoughts are as powerful as spoken words, so be careful what you think.

Let's return to Triangle's dream. She notes that one belief contains a negative—"I must not be seen"—so she changes it to "I can be seen, or it is safe to be seen." She repeats the statement with "no" at the end: "It is safe to be seen, no." If this statement tests "yes," it's true—it's not safe to be seen. If this statement tests "no," it's false—it is safe to be seen, so Triangle is safe when people see her. If she tests "yes" for both, she has dual beliefs, which we will discuss in *Dream Digging Guide 3*.

Now let's see what surprises are in store for Triangle.

Triangle tests each of the "I" statements and records her results in the "yes/no" column.

Before we go on, test yourself on Triangle's beliefs. Are any of them lurking in your subconscious mind? We share many limiting subconscious beliefs that block our progress.

Triangle looks at her results. "Now what? I don't want to be controlling and domineering, but how do I change this?" That's the topic of *Dream Digging Guide 3*.

Symbol	Description/characteristics	Feelings	"I" statements—beliefs to be verified	Yes/no
Monster	Green	Rage	I am in a rage.	Y
	Big	Wants control	I want control.	Y
		Wants to dominate	I want to dominate.	Y
		Threatening	I am domineering.	Y
		Terrified of him	I am threatening.	Y
			I am terrified of myself.	Y
Hatbox	White	Holds something precious	I am safe.	Y
		Safe	I must protect myself.	Y
		Must protect it	I must hide.	Y
		Must hide it		
Diamond	Valuable	Must not be seen	I am valuable.	Y
	Cut and polished	Love	I am polished.	Y
	Beautiful	Happy	I am beautiful.	Y
	Many facets	Proud	I have many facets.	Y
		Fear of being stolen	It is safe to be seen.	N
			It is safe to be seen, no.	Y
			I am loving.	Y
			I am happy.	Y
			I am proud.	Y
Action - Hide the diamond		Fear	I fear someone will steal from me—lose myself.	Y
		Must not be seen.	I must hide what is precious.	Y

Comparison between Individual and Group Work

This is a recording of a real dream titled *Rotten Railings*. Note the bold dream journal categories.

Date: Saturday, September 26, 2015 [always date your dreams to help recall the context, what was going on in your life at the time of the dream]

Dream:

I am on a porch with a railing (Victorian style). The part that is missing I had remade. George is finishing it.

I discover the remaining railing is rotten. I break some off in my hand. Now I have to replace the whole thing.

I am waiting for a woman consultant. I am on time, but she is busy. I wait an hour. She walks by me toward 3 women waiting for their paychecks.

She says that she'll be with me after . . .

I sternly say, "I've waited 3 hours. How fast can you write those checks?"

I knew the checks were more important to those women than my issue was to me.

Feelings while dreaming: Discouraged, fear about the condition of the porch, regret I had a part replaced. Resentful about being abused, ignored.

Context: I struggled all week to rebuild websites. I made a video, but I couldn't load it because it was too large. I was frustrated that each step seemed insurmountable. Listened to a marketing webinar and thought I did my websites all wrong.

Went to voice therapy. Voice is better, but I still don't have it back after three weeks of work. Breath is short, so my vocal function exercises don't show much progress.

Last week I found out that one front tooth might be descending because there is a problem with the root canal. Worst case scenario might involve an implant. I worried about cost. All this was caused by a complication with a medical test designed to be preventive. But I incurred more damage at the time and still am paying eleven years later.

Fear of spending too much on my business. I take one step which leads to another thing and another and another that needs to be fixed. When will it all be fixed: websites, teeth, voice? (3 things!)

Note: As I wrote the context, what was going on in my life at the time of the dream, some of the metaphors' meanings became clear.

Here is the dream again, with the metaphors in bold print. Actions are metaphors also:

> I am on a **porch** with a **railing** (Victorian style). The **part that is missing** I had **remade. George is finishing it.**
>
> I discover the **remaining railing is rotten. I break some off** in my hand. Now I **have to replace the whole thing.**
>
> I am **waiting** for a **woman consultant.** I am on time, but she **is busy. I wait an hour.** She **walks by me** toward **3 women waiting** for their **paychecks.**
>
> She says that she'll be with me **after** . . .
>
> I sternly say, "I've **waited 3 hours. How fast** can you **write those checks?"**
>
> I knew the **checks were more important** to those women **than my issue was to me.**

Now it is time to list those metaphors on a chart and ascribe characteristics and feeling to each. Here is the first scene:

Metaphor	Characteristics	Feelings
Porch	Wooden Brown Victorian style	Love porches Outside but protected Comfort
Victorian railing	Old-fashioned Hand rail Requires a lot of work for upkeep	Exhausting
Rotten railing	No support No protection from falling off porch	Regret that things are deteriorating Fear of not being able to fix it
Missing part	The part I thought needed repair Section of hand railing	Sad: useless now that it couldn't be attached
George	Brother, his age now	Always there
Remade	Do over, repair	Tired of always doing it over
Finishing it	The action that makes it like new	Finishing a repair would feel good, but this can't be attached, is meaningless, sad
George finishing it	He is always fixing things for other people	Wish I could do it myself

Note. The consultant part of the dream didn't make sense, so I ignored it.

Because our dream images and metaphors are parts of ourselves, take each characteristic and feeling to make "I" statements: statements about yourself. Remember the language of the subconscious:

- no double meanings, jokes;
- no negatives—rephrase to use "without" or put "no" at the end of the statement;
- no "can" or "try";
- present tense—no future tense.

Here are my statements for "porch." I let the ideas bubble up. In a theta brain wave, I let my subconscious help me with these statements:

1. I am wooden—inflexible.
2. I protect others.
3. I protect myself.
4. I am outside.
5. I am an outsider.
6. I am an insider.
7. I am safe outside.
8. I am comfortable.

For "railing":

1. I am old-fashioned.
2. I require a lot of upkeep.
3. I am exhausting to others.
4. I am exhausting to myself.
5. I am exhausted.

For "rotten railing":

1. I have support.
2. I have support, no. I am without support.
3. I accept support.
4. I know whom to trust for support.
5. I am rotten.
6. I can be fixed.
7. I can be fixed, no.

8. I am beyond hope—an idea that just came as I was writing.

Now I muscle test to see which beliefs are actually in my subconscious. Some of them will be; others won't be there. Sometimes I will have both the positive and negative versions, dual beliefs. Some beliefs are positive that I want to keep.

You get the idea. You have probably noticed connections between the context and the images in the dreams:

- body that needs attention and the feelings around that;
- "three" as in three weeks of voice exercises;
- no complete "payoff" (checks) in sight;
- when will everything be fixed?

I took this dream to my dream group. With their help, I added the **ideas in bold print.**

Metaphor	Characteristics	Feelings
Porch	Wooden Brown Victorian style **Entrance** **Place of social interaction** **exposed**	Love porches Outside but protected Comfort
Victorian railing	Old-fashioned Hand rail— **protection** Requires a lot of work for upkeep **Carefully crafted**	Exhausting **Indignant** **Exposed**
Rotten railing	No support No protection from falling off porch **Disintegrating**	Regret that things are deteriorating Fear of not being able to fix it **Anger** **Disappointment** **Loss—sad**
Missing part	The part I thought needed repair Section of hand railing	Sad: useless now that it couldn't be attached **Failure**
George	Brother, his age now	Always there

Metaphor	Characteristics	Feelings
Remade	Do over, repair	Tired of always doing it over **Waste of time** **Anger—delegating isn't working** **Not going as planned**
Finishing it	The action that makes it like new	Finishing a repair would feel good, but this can't be attached, is meaningless, sad
George finishing it	He is always fixing things for other people	Wish I could do it myself
3 (dentists = consultants)	**Consulted 3 dentists** **3 options** **3 hours—long wait**	**Dentists** **– 1st, not smart enough** **– 2nd, out of her depth** **– 3rd, competent**
3 options	**Best option is most expensive**	**I can afford it.** **I am worth an implant.** **I resent the money going to the implant.** **I must give up vacation for dental work.** **I must give up joy for dental work.**
Consultant	**Need consultants** **– dental work** **– web work** **Cold and distant**	**Not good enough myself** **Resent asking for help**
Waiting **Time is broken: 1 hour turns to 3 hours**	**I run out of time** **Can't meet my goals on my timeline** **I exaggerate.**	**Disappointment** **Resentment**
Give up place	**I am ignored.** **I am abused.** **I put others' needs before mine.**	**Anger** **Resentment**
Checks	**Checking on things** **Money**	**Resent the money for the implant** **Resent spending to take care of my needs**

Messages discovered in the dream group:

1. The railing is like my front teeth—part of them have been replaced, part of them need replacing. It presents the "entrance" of my appearance, the first impression.

2. Consultants: I need consultants for my dental work and my web work.
3. "3": I had three dental consultants at the time of the dream. I had three web consultants. I had three weeks of voice exercise lessons without much progress.

Now I have additional beliefs to be verified. Not all will test positive:

1. I am old.
2. I require upkeep.
3. I am carefully crafted.
4. I am exposed.
5. I am disintegrating.
6. I am falling apart.
7. I am a failure.
8. I am a disappointment to myself.
9. I am a waste of time.
10. I resent the time it takes to care for myself.
11. I resent the time it takes to nurture myself.
12. I resent the time it takes to nurture myself first.
13. I am impatient.
14. I nurture myself first.
15. I deserve to nurture myself first.
16. I exaggerate my needs.
17. I give up my place.
18. I am ignored.
19. I am abused.
20. I put others' needs before mine.
21. I know when to put others first (yes), and I do (no).
22. My needs are a waste of time.
23. My social presence is disintegrating.
24. My appearance is disintegrating.
25. Delegation works.
26. It's safe to delegate.
27. I know to whom to delegate.
28. I know when to delegate.
29. My needs are met.
30. My needs are met, no.

31. I deserve to meet my needs.
32. I deserve to nurture myself.
33. I took a vow to be perfect.
34. I am perfect the way I am.
35. I deserve help.
36. Accepting help diminishes me.
37. I am worth spending money on myself.
38. Implants are worth the money.
39. I am smart enough.
40. I am out of my depth—competency.
41. I am competent.
42. I can afford the best dental work.
43. I am worth an implant.
44. I resent the money going to the implant.
45. I must give up vacation for dental work.
46. I must give up joy for dental work.
47. I took a vow to give up joy.
48. I resent asking for help.
49. I resent spending money on my needs (dental work).
50. I am good enough.
51. I ignore myself.
52. I abuse myself.
53. I am a powerful consultant.
54. I know when to check on things.
55. I do check on things.

Impact of the Dream Group

By myself, I wasn't motivated to look at the last half of the dream. Of course, the dream group wouldn't let me get away with this! Their discussion helped me find deeper and multiple meanings of the metaphors. For example, I would never have appreciated the associations made with "3"—three dentists, three dental consultations, waiting one hour that turned into three hours, leading to finding that I believe I am impatient. The porch is a stand-in for my smile. It gives first impressions, so I want it to look the best. The railing might be a metaphor for the row of front teeth, one of which needs an implant. The other front tooth already is an implant. I was also able to find at least fifty-five more beliefs hidden in the metaphors.

Precognition?

Three months later, I realized I needed three crowns on my worn bottom front teeth. Was this the porch railing metaphor? At the time of the dream, I only noticed two bottom teeth that needed crowns. However, the dentist said all three needed crowns—and I had consulted three dentists before I started the work. How clever is the dreaming mind! You can only appreciate the ingenuity of your subconscious, dreaming mind if you record your dreams and revisit your dream journal.

Your Turn

You get the idea. Now it's your turn. Use the template in Appendix B to record a dream. Then use the chart in Appendix C to verify subconscious beliefs. Remember, muscle testing only indicates what your subconscious believes; it does not necessarily indicate the "truth." Not all the potential beliefs will test positive. Some beliefs you will want to keep. But some of our beliefs impede us, so it's important to learn what impedes us. You might be surprised what you learn about yourself.

Online dream groups that use the complete Ullman method are available at http://courses.dreamdigging.net/.

ten

~))⌒~

The Big Noise, Faulty Beliefs, and Grandpa

The Big Noise

Remember that noise I kept hearing both in waking life and in my dreams as a child? I asked my father, but he thought it was the tractor or the field chopper. After I had completed the first five weeks of hypnotherapy training fifty years later, I became intrigued by Michael Newton's (2006) *Life between Lives: Hypnotherapy for Spiritual Regression*. Because I lived in New York City, I easily found several practitioners and trainers from the Newton Institute. One was Paul Aurand, a certified hypnotherapist and lead trainer for the Newton Institute who had also survived a lightning strike (Aurand 1998). I really wanted to have a series of sessions with him. As they were quite expensive, I settled for one that included a regression and meeting of my angels.

During the session and in a theta state, I finally arrived at the life previous to this one. I was a boy about eight years old in a building with huge doors. My parents had told me under no circumstances was I to leave that building. I turned away from the door and faced a bombed-out wall. I escaped over the pile of rubble only to see a train leaving with my parents and relatives. I ran to catch them because I didn't want to be alone. Little did I know then that they were going to Auschwitz. Now I understood that loud noise and big hole in the ground. I was killed by an earth mover that shoved us into the hole. In retrospect, I now know why I had sobbed uncontrollably as I had watched Jews getting on the trains in *Schindler's List*.

Faulty Beliefs

The first time I attempted a past-life regression, I felt I had failed to find answers why my marriage was in trouble. The hypnotherapist only said, "The problems you are facing in this life are caused by a faulty belief system." This made no sense—until I went to the ThetaHealing Institute of Knowledge. We learned how to find subconscious beliefs that were blocking our lives and replace them. We all have hundreds, even thousands, of unknown beliefs. We learned to "dig" to find the bottom belief that was supporting a host of other beliefs. To this day, I continue to find beliefs that sabotage me. So perhaps the hypnotherapist was right: my problems in this life are caused by all these faulty beliefs. Now I know how to find and change them.

Grandpa

I also found out why I saw my deceased grandfather on the street. One of the exercises in Basic ThetaHealing was to speak with people who had passed over—if they weren't too busy! We chose partners. One would tell whom to contact; the other would "go up" into a theta brain wave and ask to speak with the deceased person. When it was my turn, I asked my partner to contact my grandpa and ask why he appeared to me on the street two weeks after he died. She made the contact and described him to be certain she had the right person. She gave details about how he played with us when we were kids. When she asked him why he appeared to me, he said, "I wanted her to tell the rest of the family that I was okay."

"Well, that didn't work! I was so shocked, I wouldn't tell anybody!" I said.

"Yes, she is a little slow sometimes," he joked.

Perhaps he was right. It did take me a few decades to solve these mysteries!

You are now ready to begin your journey. Record your dreams consistently. Identify the metaphors, their characteristics and feelings. Turn these into "I" statements. These are potential subconscious beliefs. If you are a certified ThetaHealer, you have the skills to change beliefs that no longer serve you. If you want to become a ThetaHealer, go to http://www.thetahealing.com/ to find classes and certified practitioners.

Appendix A
Dream Group Participant Guide

Based on the work of Montague (Monte) Ullman, MD

Purpose

The purpose of a dream group is to help the dreamer explore the meaning of dream metaphors. This group exists for the benefit of the dreamer, not for the benefit of group members, although that is often an outcome. Furthermore, the dream group does not provide therapy, even though the process might be therapeutic.

Safety Factor

A dreamer creates images and scenarios during sleep that would not appear during waking life. We are always editing and revising during waking life to put on our "best public face." Dream metaphors tell the unedited, unrevised truth about us. Rest assured, no one dreams of things she is not ready to confront. However, it is somewhat intimidating to share a dream publicly. Therefore, when a person chooses to share a dream, he is lowering defenses with a group whose responsibility is to ensure the safety of the dreamer. Safety guidelines of the Ullman process are as follows:

- The dreamer controls the process.
- The dreamer's privacy is not invaded.
- Leading questions are not allowed.
- The dreamer always determines the level of sharing.
- The dreamer can terminate the process at any point.
- No content of the dream group can be shared with people outside the group.
- Confidentiality must be maintained.

Listening Skills

- No suggestions
- No interrupting the dreamer

Questioning Skills

- No leading questions; say, "Can you say anything more about . . . ?"
- No information-demanding questions
- No topics not initiated by the dreamer

Process

To preserve the dreamer's safety and yet help discover the meaning of the dream, Monte designed a highly structured process.

Stage I

1. If two or more people want to share, they decide among themselves who will share.
2. *The dream*: The dreamer reads or tells the dream slowly as the group writes it down verbatim.
3. *Clarifying questions*: facts in the dream
   a. Who or what is real in waking life?
   b. What were the feelings in the dream—while dreaming?
   c. What were the ages and relationships of characters in the dream?

Stage II

1. *The game*: Without looking at the dreamer, the group talks about the dream as if it were their own:
   a. By exploring their own feelings: "If it were my dream, I would feel . . ."
   b. By exploring the metaphors: "If it were my dream, going to my aunt's house means a lot of conflict."

Stage III

1. *Dreamer responds*: The dream is returned to the dreamer with the invitation to respond without interruption in any way he wishes. The dreamer can share the validity of the comments made in Stage II.
2. *Context*: The group, with the dreamer's permission, asks general questions about the recent events that constitute the context of the dream, which may help the dreamer make further associations. Each person is unique; therefore, the dream images emerge out of the unique life experience, usually some recent events and feelings.
3. *Playback*: The dream is read back to the dreamer (change "I" to "you") scene by scene, to help the dreamer focus on elements still to be explored. With the additional data provided by the group, the dreamer may be able to clarify images.
4. *Orchestration*: With the dreamer's permission, the group offers further connections between what the dreamer has stated but has not connected. These are new connections, not made by the dreamer, based on what the dreamer has said. It is not the time to bring in outside information and apply it to the dream.

Stage IV

- The dreamer has the *final word*. The dreamer is invited to share any insights about the dream or the work the group did with the dream.
- At the next dream session, the dreamer is invited to share further insights.

Monte's papers can be found at http://siivola.org/monte.

Appendix B
Dream Journal Template

Date _____   **Day** _____

Title (optional): _____

Feelings and Thoughts upon Drifting to Sleep: _____
_____
_____

Dream: _____
_____
_____
_____
_____
_____
_____
_____

Feelings in the Dream (while dreaming): _____
_____

Context (events and emotions/feelings prior to the dream): ____
_____
_____
_____
_____
_____

Appendix C
Metaphor–Belief Template

1. Identify the metaphors: images and actions.
2. Describe each metaphor.
3. Find the feeling of each metaphor. Start with sad, mad, glad, and afraid.
4. Make "I" statements from each characteristic and feeling to verify beliefs.
5. Record result in the "yes/no" column.

A template is provided on the following page.

Metaphors—Beliefs

Metaphor	Description/characteristics	Feelings	"I" statements—beliefs to be verified	Yes/no

References

Aurand, Paul. 1998. An en-lightning experience. New York City, July 17. http://www.holistichealingcenter.com/adventures1.html (accessed September 23, 2016).

Barrett, Deirdre. 2001. *The Committee of Sleep: How Artists, Scientists, and Athletes Use Dreams or Creative Problem-Solving—and How You Can Too.* New York: Crown.

Boxer, S. 2001. Ideas and trends: The banality of terror; dreams of holy war over a quiet evening. *New York Times,* December 16. http://www.nytimes.com/2001/12/16/weekinreview/ideas-trends-the-banality-of-terror-dreams-of-holy-war-over-a-quiet-evening .html (accessed July 27, 2016).

Braden, Gregg. 2007. *The Divine Matrix.* Carlsbad, Calif.: Hay House.

Burch, Wanda E. 2003. *She Who Dreams: A Journey into Healing through Dreamwork.* Novato, Calif.: New World Library.

Cowgil, Charles. 1997. Carl Jung. http://www.muskingum .edu/~psych/psycweb/history/jung.htm (accessed July 26, 2015).

Dement, W. C., and N. Kleitman. 1957. Cyclic variations in EEG during sleep and their relation to eye movements, body motility and dreaming. *Clinical Neurophysiology* 9: 673–90.

Freudenrich, Craig, and Robynne Boyd. n.d. How your brain works. http://science.howstuffworks.com/life/inside-the-mind/human-brain/brain.htm (accessed July 13, 2015).

Hillman, Keith. 2014. An introduction to the different types of brainwave and what they mean. November 10. http://www .psychology24.org/an-introduction-to-the-different-types-of-brainwave-and-what-they-mean/ (accessed June 19, 2016).

Hobson, J. Allan. 2015. *Psychodynamic Neurology.* Boca Raton, Fla.: CRC Press.

James, Matthew B. 2013. Conscious of the unconscious: Work with your unconscious, rather than trying to browbeat it into submission. *Psychology Today,* July 30. https://www.psychologytoday.com/blog/focus-forgiveness/201307/conscious-the-unconscious (accessed July 26, 2015).

Lewis, Penelope A. 2014. What is dreaming and what does it tell us about memory? *Scientific American,* July 18. http://www.scientificamerican.com/article/what-is-dreaming-and-what-does-it-tell-us-about-memory-excerpt/ (accessed May 16, 2016).

Lipton, Bruce H. 2005. *The Biology of Belief: Unleashing the Power of Consciousness, Matter, and Miracles.* Santa Rosa, Calif.: Elite Books.

————. 2016. *The Biology of Belief: Unleash the Power of Your Mind to Take Control of Your Life.* Carlsbad, Calif.: Hay House Online Learning.

Llinas, Rodolfo. n.d. Brainwave frequency listing: Cycles per second (HERTZ) . . . correspondences to mental states, physiology, colors, notes and planets. http://www.bibliotecapleyades.net/ciencia/ciencia_cambio06a.htm (accessed June 20, 2015).

Luborsky, Ellen B., Maureen O'Reilly-Landry, and Jacob A. Arlow. 2010. Psychoanalysis. In *Current Psychotherapies,* ed. Raymond J. Corsini and Danny Wedding, 16–24. Belmont, Calif.: Brooks/Cole/Cengage Learning.

Lukeman, Alex. 2011. *What Your Dreams Can Teach You: A Handbook for Dreamers.* Kindle.

Lyons, T. 2012. *Dreams and Guided Imagery: Gifts for Transforming Illness and Crisis.* Bloomington, Ind.: Balboa Press.

McLeod, S. A. 2013. Sigmund Freud. http://www.simplypsychology.org/Sigmund-Freud.html (accessed July 26, 2015).

Mental Health Daily. 2014. 5 types of brain waves frequencies: Gamma, beta, alpha, theta, delta. April 15. http://mentalhealthdaily.com/2014/04/15/5-types-of-brain-waves-frequencies-gamma-beta-alpha-theta-delta/ (accessed July 13, 2015).

Newton, Michael. 2006. *Life between Lives: Hypnotherapy for Spiritual Regression.* Woodbury, Minn.: Llewellyn.

O'Keefe-Kanavos, K. 2014. *Surviving Cancerland: Intuitive Aspects of Healing.* Fort Bragg, Calif.: Cypress House.

Otto, R. n.d. *The Complete Weight Loss Specialty Certification Course.* Laceyville, Pa.

Pert, Candace. 1999. *Molecules of Emotion: The Science behind Mind–Body Medicine.* New York: Touchstone.

Psychology World. n.d. Stages of sleep. http://web.mst .edu/~psyworld/sleep_stages.htm#1a (accessed July 22, 2015).

Robinson, Jennifer. 2014. What are REM and non-REM sleep? October 22. http://www.webmd.com/sleep-disorders/guide/ sleep-101 (accessed July 7, 2015).

Siegel, Daniel J. 2011. *Mindsight: The New Science of Personal Transformation.* New York: Bantam.

Siivola, Markku. 2008. *Understanding Dreams: The Gateway to Dreams without Dream Interpretation.* Trans. Richard Jenkins and Markku Siivola. New York: Cosimo Books.

Simmerman, Tim. 2007. *Medical Hypnotherapy: Principles and Methods of Practice.* Vol. 1. Santa Fe, N.M.: Peaceful Planet Press.

Staroversky, Ivan. 2013. Three minds: Conscious vs subconscious vs unconscious. May 23. https://staroversky.com/blog/ three-minds-conscious-subconscious-unconscious (accessed September 28, 2015).

Stibal, Vianna. 2014. ThetaHealing general FAQs. May 22. http:// thetahealing.com/thetahealing-questions.html (accessed May 2014, 2014).

———. 2015. ThetaHealing: Spiritual, physical, emotional well-being. February 12. http://www.thetahealing.com/thetahealing-questions.html (accessed February 12, 2015).

Susmakova, K. 2004. Human sleep and sleep EEG. *Measurement Science Review* 4, no. 2: 59–72. http://www.measurement. sk/2004/S2/susmakova.pdf (accessed September 23, 2016).

Transparent Corporation. n.d. Brainwaves overview. http://www .transparentcorp.com/products/np/brainwaves.php (accessed July 14, 2015).

Ullman, Montague. 1996. *Appreciating Dreams: A Group Approach.* Thousand Oaks, Calif.: Sage.

———. 1999. The experiential dream group. In *The Variety of Dream Experience: Expanding Our Ways of Working with Dreams,* ed. Montague Ullman and Claire Limmer, 13–19. Albany: State University of New York Press.

———. 2001. A note on the social referents of dreams. *Dreaming* 11, no. 1 (2001).

Wagner, S. 2015. Visions of the 9/11 attack. October 29. http://
paranormal.about.com/od/prophetsandprophecies/a/Visions-
Of-The-9-11-Attack.htm (accessed July 27, 2016).
Westminster College. n.d. The measurement of brainwaves. http://
www.psych.westminster.edu/psybio/BN/Labs/Brainwaves.htm
(accessed July 13, 2015).
Wren, Kathleen. 2001. How the brain turns reality into dreams.
Science Mysteries on NBCNEWS.com, October 12. http://www
.nbcnews.com/id/3077505#.Via_MPmht7c (accessed October
20, 2015).

Online Resources

The Lucidity Institute, *NightLight,* NL1.1, http://www.lucidity.com/
NL11.DreamRecall.html

How to Remember Dreams, http://www.wikihow.com/

International Association for the Study of Dreams, http://www
.asdreams.org/

Online dream groups that use the Ullman Method: http://www
.courses.dreamdigging.net/

ThetaHealing, http://www.thetahealing.com/ and http://www
.mindbalance.biz/

Acknowledgments

I am deeply indebted to many people who assisted with this manuscript. My writing critique groups helped me clarify salient points. They patiently read and reread my work: Sandra Lapham, Paula Schwartz, Barbara Warne, Diane Schmidt, Wally Gordon, Chris Enke, Kevin Getchell, Havva Houshmand, Nadine Takahashi, John Wymore, and Raul Araujo. ThetaHealing colleague Debbie Steg provided invaluable advice along with a continual supply of humorous life stories.

My editor and page designer, Holly T. Monteith, and cover designer, Scarlett Rugers, were indispensable to the publishing process.

Michael Espinoza's readings provided encouragement, direction, and laughter on the darkest of days.

Janet Wahl, PhD, CHt, began her career as a teacher. After earning her PhD in Language, Literacy, and Learning, she served as a special education director and consultant, assistant professor, and assistant superintendent for curriculum and instruction. During fifteen years of that time, she participated in Montague Ullman's dream groups and took his leadership training workshops. After retirement, she studied hypnotherapy and ThetaHealing. As a ThetaHealing Master, she combined the ThetaHealing technique with dream work. She currently sees clients and teaches courses in dream work and ThetaHealing. She is the author of *Dream Digging Guide 1: Discover the Messages in Your Dreams with the Ullman Method.*

CPSIA information can be obtained
at www.ICGtesting.com
Printed in the USA
FSOW02n2226120117
29599FS